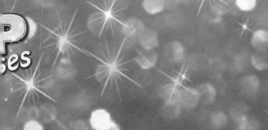

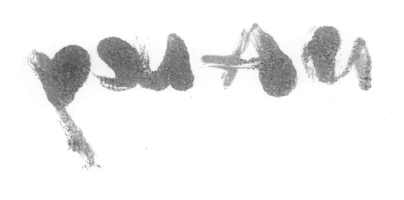

POP princesses
ANNUAL 2013

This Annual belongs to

....

Pop Princesses Annual 2013

Contents

First published in the UK in 2012
By Instinctive Product Development

© Instinctive Product Development 2012 under license from Universal Music TV a division of Universal Music Operations Limited 2012

Printed and bound in China

ISBN: 978-1-908816-17-7

Images courtesy of PA Photos and Shutterstock

With special thanks to Keeley and Madelaine Gardner, Sharon French, Sarah-Jane Garner.

Credits:
Written by Vanessa Gardner
with Rebecca Ellis.

Reality TV Pop Princesses

Pop Princesses are more popular than ever and have taken over our TVs appearing in our favourite reality TV shows. Here are some of the princesses to look out for.

Jessie J

Show: The Voice UK
Role: Coach
Style: Sassy, cool and an amazing voice!
Twitter: @JessieJ

"It's so important to work hard for your success! Earn it, celebrate it and love it!"

Tulisa

Show: The X Factor
Role: Judge/Mentor
Style: Outspoken, street smart and the female boss!
Twitter: @OfficialTulisa

"I'm growing as a person, so you might see a change in me simply because I'm growing up but I'm just going to be me!"

Jennifer Lopez

Show: American Idol
Role: Judge
Style: Style queen, caring and approachable.
Twitter: @JLo
"It hasn't changed. I'm still an emotional person."

Alesha Dixon

Show: Britain's Got Talent
Role: Judge
Style: Loud, extrovert and with a mad laugh!
Twitter: @AleshaOfficial
"I want the person that wins to be the act that catches the heart of the British public."

The Saturdays

Show: 24/7
Role: Reality show stars!
Style: Behind the scenes fun and a peek into the girls' real lives!
Twitter: @TheSaturdays
Pop Princess Fact: Just signed up for a new MTV reality show.

Living the Pop Princess Life

Katy Perry
Sunglasses needed!

Selena Gomez
So Cute.

Living the life of a Pop Princess is not as easy as it looks! Wearing the latest fashions from daring dresses to platform shoes takes tons of planning. Sometimes it works and sometimes it doesn't but that is why we love them! Let's take a look at how some of our favourite stars carry off the latest looks - help us decide if you love it or hate it!

So Cool!

Alexandra Burke
Oops!

Florence Welch
Flower Power!

LOL

Pixie Lott
What a cute bag!

Lady Gaga
Hats off to Gaga!

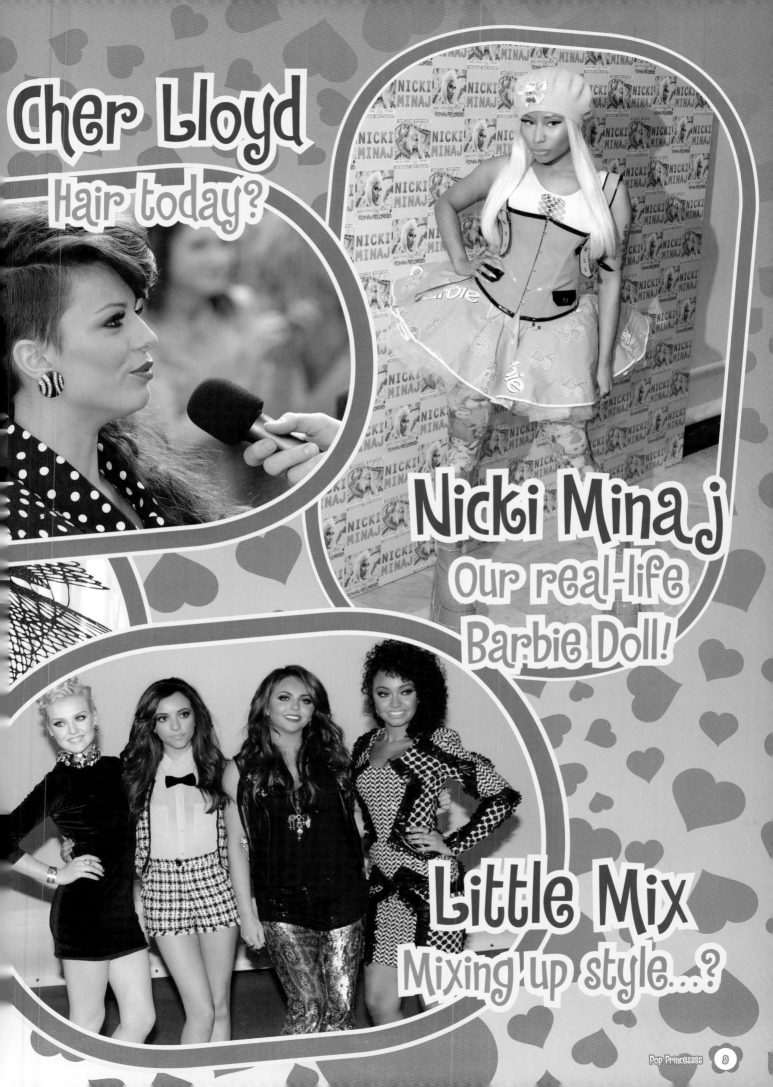

Cher Lloyd
Hair today?

Nicki Minaj
Our real-life Barbie Doll!

Little Mix
Mixing up style...?

The Wacky World of Jessie J

Jessie J arrives at The BRITs!

Wearing her trademark wild print...

The famous catsuit!

Since Jessie J shot to superstardom with Do It Like a Dude and Price Tag we have all been mesmerised by her quirky and individual style. The only female UK artist to have six Top 10 singles off one album she is surely here to stay and entertain us with more wild outfits and crazy hair!

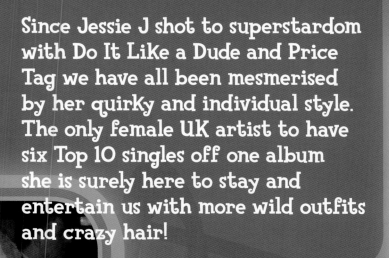

Even with an injured foot Jessie is at her most stylish.

On the red carpet with a different look.

Looking a little bit scary but fab!

Demi Lovato

FACTFILE

Birthday: 20th August 1992

TV Shows: Barney & Friends, As the Bell Rings, Sonny With A Chance, Just Jordan (Guest Star), Prison Break (Guest Star)

Movies: Camp Rock, Princess Protection Program (TV Movies)

Instruments: Demi plays the guitar, piano and drums!

BFF: Selena Gomez

Did You Know: Demi has a long tongue which she can touch her nose with, but is also very flexible and can put her feet behind her head. Ouch!

Cher Lloyd

Knock Before You Enter

ROOM

The Great British Cupcake

- Preheat the oven to 180°C (Electric fan oven 160°C | Gas Mark 4) and put 12 paper cases into a baking tray. (Top Tip: You can also use silicone cupcake cases!)
- Beat the butter and sugar until very light and fluffy.
- Add the eggs one at a time, beating each one in well before adding the next. Add the vanilla essence.
- Fold in the flour and baking powder.
- Bake in the oven for 10-20 minutes approx.
- When cooked remove from the oven and cool whilst you make the topping.
- Beat the butter and icing sugar together in a bowl.
- Add the hot water and beat until smooth.
- Add your chosen food colourings then ice the top of your cupcakes, adding decorations to finish.

INGREDIENTS

- 100g butter or margarine
- 100g caster sugar
- 100g self-raising flour, sifted
- 2 eggs
- 1/4 teaspoon baking powder (optional)
- 1/2 teaspoon vanilla essence (optional)

FOR THE TOPPING

- 250g icing sugar
- 150g softened butter
- 2 teaspoons hot water (not boiling)

FOR DECORATION

- Red, white, blue sprinkles

Safety Tip: Always get an adult to help when you are using the hob or oven!

YUM-YUM!

Selena Gomez
DID YOU KNOW

Selena turned down a role in High School Musical 3.

She started acting at the age of seven on the show Barney & Friends.

Selena loves Snickers.

The name Selena means 'Moon' in Greek.

Her Twitter name is **@selenagomez**

Selena wears Size 7 shoes (4½ UK).

She starred as Alex Russo in Wizards of Waverly Place on the Disney Channel.

Selena loves wearing Converse shoes.

Selena plays the guitar, piano and drums.

Her starsign is Cancer.

Who's iN and Who's

Rihanna

With her ever-changing hair and top pop tunes Rihanna is bigger and better than ever! Now starring in movies she is a true Pop Princess!

Tulisa

Tulisa is going solo and with a new album and after winning her debut season of The X Factor she is sure to become a superstar this year!

Cheryl

After some much-needed time off Cheryl is back with a new album and a rumoured Girls Aloud reunion. We can't wait!

Definitely OUT!

Ellie Goulding

Her face says it all. Ellie has been overtaken by her rivals but we're sure she will be back!

Ke$ha

What has happened to Ke$ha this year? We're not sure where she's at!

Nicole Scherzinger

Not a great year for Nicole having been sacked from The X Factor USA, and little chart success!

POP PARTY

Presents

A BRAND NEW ALBUM

featuring the cutest boys in the charts.

Plus a bonus double sided poster and Bonus DVD!

Pop Princesses Wordsearch

```
D Z C T F O G X X S T G J
E A C I D Y G R H S I C P
R D N E B I H U D D X V K
L Q E C A L K C E N Z G A
I R Y G E K B Y X E O J J
P M X O T A V O L I M E D
G J Q K V C F P X R T I R
L P R I N C E S S F U S O
O D V G U K A Z D T L S T
S A E L O K L D F S I E C
S R C B F A L T H E S J A
Q J V Y X D H W G B A N F
S U Y S A T U R D A Y S X
```

Try and find:

Best Friends

Dance

Demi Lovato

Jessie J

Lip Gloss

Necklace

Princess

Saturdays

Tulisa

X Factor

Answers:

```
X S A T U R D A Y S
N B B G W H D X Y V U
A S J S T L A F B J
C E I T F L O K L E C R
T S U L S Z K U G V D A
R S I R F X X V C K R G
O I M I L O V A T O X L
D E M E X Y B K E G J R
J G Z N E C A L K C E Y M
Y V D U H R G Y D I Y K
P C I X Y D I C A B
J G T F O G X X T C Z D
```

COOKIE

Ingredients:

- 100g/3½oz unsalted butter or cooking margarine
- 100g/3½oz caster sugar
- 1 egg, lightly beaten
- 275g/10oz plain flour
- 1 teaspoon vanilla extract

For decoration:

- 400g/14oz icing sugar
- 3-4 tablespoons water
- 2-3 drops food colourings

Step by Step:

- Preheat the oven to 190C/375F/Gas 5.
- Line a baking tray with greaseproof paper.
- Cream the butter and sugar together in a bowl until light and fluffy!
- Beat in the egg and vanilla extract, a little at a time, until mixed.
- Stir in the flour until the mixture comes together as a dough.
- Roll the dough out on a lightly-floured work surface with a rolling pin.
- Using cookie cutters, cut cookies out of the dough and carefully place onto the baking tray.
- Bake the biscuits for 8-10 minutes, or until golden brown. Set aside to cool down and then remove onto a wire rack.

yum-yum

Top Tip: Don't use too much colouring or the colours will be too bright!

CRAZY

Top Tip: Use different shaped cutters for a mix n match look!

Decorating the cookies is the fun bit. There are lots of ways to decorate – use the basic recipe but add your own ideas too!

- For the icing, sift the icing sugar into a large mixing bowl and stir in enough water to create a smooth mixture. Stir in the food colouring.

- Carefully spread the icing onto the biscuits using a knife.

- Decorate with sprinkles or other iced decorations! Set aside until the icing hardens.

Top Tip: A tiny bit of red colouring makes a light pink princess colour!

MAKE YOUR OWN SWEETS

Yummy Chocolate Truffles!

Makes: Up to 30 sweets.

- 5 tablespoons double cream
- 100g unsalted butter, cubed, or cooking margarine
- 300g dark chocolate, at least 70% cocoa, chopped
- 5 tablespoons cocoa powder

Top Tip: Use a teaspoon to help you roll the mixture into balls.

Step by Step:

- Heat the cream in a saucepan until it comes to a simmer.
- Add the butter and stir until it has melted.
- Add the chopped chocolate and stir until it melts.
- Remove from heat and pour the mixture into a dish.
- Chill in the fridge for at least two hours, until it is firm to touch.
- Roll the mixture into small balls no bigger than 3cms.
- Roll each ball into the cocoa powder carefully or decorate your truffle using sprinkles or edible decorations.

Safety Tip:
Always get an adult to help when you are using the hob or oven!

Top Tip:
Store in the fridge in an airtight box for up to 2 weeks.

Songs You Might Know

★★★★★★★★★★★★★★★★★★★

Guess which Pop Princesses sang these songs (answers below).

1. Quitting's out of the question

2. It's not about the money, money, money

3. I want your drama, the touch of your hand

4. You can't stop clickin about me

5. Sometimes it lasts in love but sometimes it hurts instead

★★★★★★★★★★★★★★★★★★★

5. Adele – Someone Like You

4. Cher Lloyd – Swagger Jagger

3. Lady Gaga – Bad Romance

2. Jessie J – Price Tag

1. Cheryl Cole – Fight For This Love

Lady Gaga

DID YOU KNOW

Lady Gaga used to write songs for The Pussycat Dolls.

Her stage name of "Lady Gaga" comes from the Queen song Radio Gaga.

Gaga's first single Just Dance went to Number 1 in five countries.

Lady Gaga's birth name is Stefani Joanne Angelina Germanotta.

Lady Gaga started playing piano at the age of 4!

Gaga designs or co-designs most of her crazy stage clothes with the "House of Gaga".

She once ordered $1000 worth of pizza for fans waiting for her outside a signing.

Her favourite song on the album Fame was Paparazzi.

Before performing she likes to have a cup of tea.

The album Born this Way has sold over 5 million copies worldwide!

The Saturdays

Jessie J

Little Mix

Make Your Own Heart Keyring

So Cool!

This is a fabulous heart keyring, which you can make as a gift for your mum, friends or keep for yourself! You can adapt the look of it by choosing your own colours and accessories. Remember you may need some help cutting the fabric, so don't forget to ask!

Materials List:

- 7cm x 7cm coloured felt
- 7cm x 7cm patterned fabric
- Keyring loop
- Buttons
- 14cm ribbon 1cm thick
- 4 strips fabric 2cm x 7cm
- Pinking shears/scissors
- Matching thread/needles

Step by Step:

Choose matching fabrics, felts and ribbons for this keyring.
The brightest coloured felt should be sandwiched between the layers of fabric.

1. Draw a heart onto a white piece of paper in pencil. (Tracing paper if you have it!)
2. Cut the heart out and use as a template.
3. Using the template, place onto your chosen fabric and cut out 2 hearts in felt and 3 hearts in fabric. Cut out one mini heart shape..
4. Using just the top chosen fabric heart, place the mini heart into the middle. Pin in place and sew on. Add the button and sew.
5. Position the ribbon in a cross shape, pin and sew.
6. Iron flat, trim using the pinking shears or scissors.
7. Sandwich the fabrics together using the bright felt in the middle.
8. Using the small strip of ribbon, make a loop and push this into the sandwiched hearts.
9. Sew around the edge of the heart 1cm from the edge.
10. Now for a second line. This time another cm in from the last and go round 2-3 times.
11. The loop for the keyring is now secure.
12. Finish off with the pinking shears by trimming all the way round to give a neat cut line all round.
13. Add the metal loop to complete this little project.

Top Tip: You can buy all the materials from craft shops.

Top Tip: You can use old clothes including jeans to make a funky keyring.

Top Tip: You can choose a colour theme and get matching fabrics!

Top Tip: You can turn it into a decoration by not including the keyring loop!

My Favourite

My Favourite **Movie**

Danity

My Favourite **Game**

connect 4

My Favourite **Clothes**

leggins, polAr Bear, top, shorts & sporcaly jumpy

My Favourite **Food**

Pezza

My Favourite **Accessories**

hire thing's

Things

My Favourite Pop Princess

Selena GOmez

My Favourite **Song**

ROCK Me

My Favourite SWEETS

ranBOW sweets

My Favourite PLACE

Home

My Favourite Animal

Panda

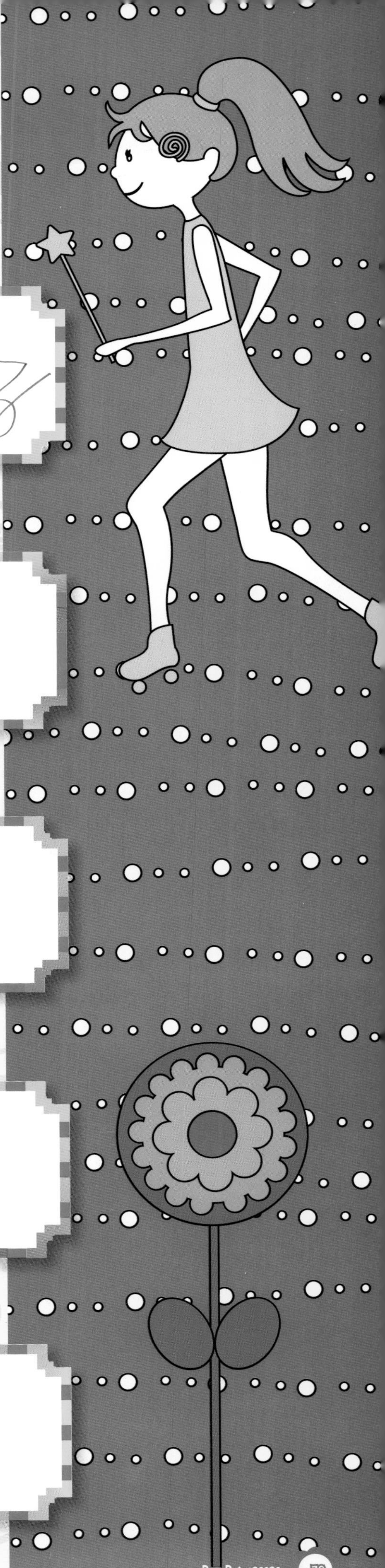

Cute Hair Tips
Triple Plait

① Make sure hair is wet and has been combed through.

② Separate hair into three separate sections.

③ Start at one end and plait first section of hair.

④ Continue to plait until all three sections are complete.

⑤ Starting at the top take each plait and plait together to create one large plait!

⑥ Add your accessory of choice once you have added a hair band to the end and look how great it looks!

Funky Curly Sideways Hair Bunch

1 Make sure your hair has been brushed thoroughly.

2 Take strands of hair on each side away from the bulk of your hair and bring to the front.

3 Carefully gather your hair and brush to one side, securing it with a hair band.

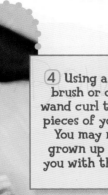

4 Using a curling brush or curling wand curl the front pieces of your hair. You may need a grown up to help you with this part!

5 It may take a while to get the perfect curl so don't give up!

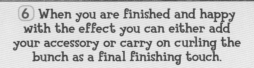

6 When you are finished and happy with the effect you can either add your accessory or carry on curling the bunch as a final finishing touch.

So Sweet

Katy Perry

fun Drinks

This tasty Chocolate Milk Float is so easy to make...

- Pour a glass of lemonade or cola but only half fill the glass!

- Using a spoon or ice-cream scoop put a helping of chocolate ice cream into the top of the glass.

- It should fizz up and makes a lovely creamy/ bubbly drink.

Yummy!

If you love raspberries this is the perfect drink for you!

- Put some fresh raspberries into the bottom of the glass.

- Pour in some raspberryade or pink lemonade – about half full.

- Using a spoon or ice-cream scoop put a helping of your favourite ice cream into the top.

- The raspberry surprise at the end is a lovely treat!

Tulisa

Best Friends Forever – Girl Bands!

Spice Girls

Viva Forever!

The Spice Girls hit worldwide fame, split-up and have since reformed for sell-out concerts. Despite Geri leaving at the height of their fame, their friendship got them back together and a new musical will celebrate the career and friendship of Victoria, Geri, Mel B, Mel C and Emma.

From the Spice Girls to The Saturdays we all love a great girl band! The friendship shared by the girls is so close because of the huge amount of time they have to spend together. We take a look at what makes girl bands so cool and why the girls are BFFs!

The Saturdays

That's So Hollywood!

With two of the band already firm friends from their days with S Club Juniors the rest of the girls that make up The Saturdays have grown together as a band, and with marriages and babies adding to the mix they will be celebrating their friendship in a new reality TV series on MTV. We can't wait!

Sugababes

So Excited!

We are so excited to hear that the original Sugababes are getting back together and are already recording music. Keisha Buchanan, Mutya Buena and Siobhán Donaghy all left the band at different times with new members joining and leaving. It was like a revolving door but news reaches us that a new album is on the way and it just shows that even if sometimes you don't get on that time heals friendships!

Girls Aloud

Something Kinda Ooooh!

Who can believe it's been 10 years since Girls Aloud were picked to be a girl band in TV show Popstars - The Rivals. We all wanted to dress like them and we loved learning the dance routines, but after a break as they all did their own thing it looks like a reunion may be coming soon. We can't wait to get on our dancing shoes!

Must-have Accessories for the Ultimate Pop Princess

So pretty!

Cute

Bling it!

Awesome

Lush

Poptastic Pop

1. Who won The X Factor in 2011?

2. How many Number 1 singles off her debut album has Jessie J had?

3. How many members of One Direction are there?

4. What girl band did Beyoncé start her pop career in?

5. Name the five members of Girls Aloud?

Princess Quiz

6. Finish this Lady Gaga song
   B _ _ _ T_ _ _ W _ _

7. How many of our Ultimate Pop Princesses (pages 54-63) are reality TV show judges?

8. Name the last Pop Princess to win The X Factor?

9. Which member of The Saturdays recently had a baby girl?

10. Who sang Starry Eyed?

Answers:

6. Born This Way
7. Two (Tulisa & Jessie J)
8. Alexandra Burke
9. Una
10. Ellie Goulding

10. Taylor Swift

Did you know Taylor Swift is very good friends with Selena Gomez? Taylor has sold an amazing 9 million digital downloads making her one of the most successful downloaded artists in the world!

Fab!

the Ultimate Pop Princess?

9. Katy Perry

One of the most hard-working Pop Princesses, Katy Perry has been on a mammoth World Tour. With her ever-changing hair colour, fantastic videos and catchy songs she has to be one of our Ultimate Pop Princesses.

WoW!

8. Demi Lovato

After appearing in Disney's Camp Rock we knew Demi had an amazing voice and it looks like she is well on the way to becoming a top Pop Princess. Her single, Skyscraper, has sold over 1 million digital copies and we think she is here to stay.

So Hip!

7. Selena Gomez

We're so sad that Wizards of Waverly Place has come to an end but so happy that we can listen to Selena singing. There are even rumours that she will release a duet with Justin Bieber.

Gorgeous!

6. Tulisa

Tulisa shot to fame with N-Dubz but has since decided to go for a solo career. Having had much success as the winning judge on The X Factor with Little Mix, she is now aiming to ride up the charts with her new album.

Lush!

5. Lady Gaga

Gaga by name and Gaga by nature. We love seeing her latest bonkers outfits but most of all we love her amazing music because she was "Born This Way". From the moment we heard Just Dance that's all we have wanted to do to the fabulous Lady Gaga's songs!

WoW!

2. Adele

Adele has become a worldwide Pop Princess sensation. Her songs are so beautiful and she always seems to pull your heartstrings with her pure voice. We love winding down to Adele songs when all you want to do is chill out to some good music.

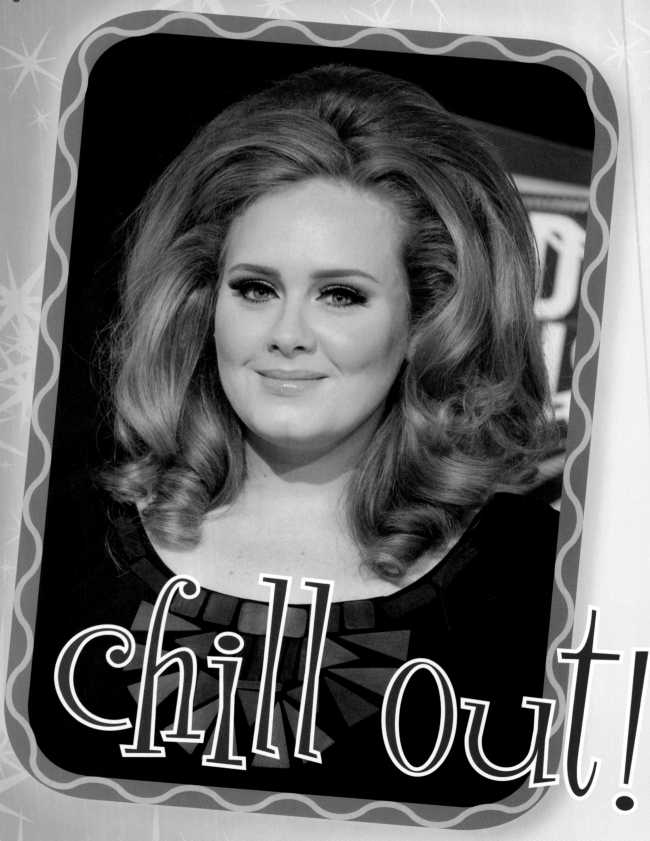

chill out!

3. Rihanna

We love her music but Rihanna is such a style icon with her ever-changing hairstyles through to her street-smart outfits. She also knows how to glam up for award shows in gorgeous outfits. We are soooo jealous!

So Cool!

2. Cheryl

The fabulous Cheryl is back with a bang with a new album called A Million Lights. Cheryl was our favourite member of Girls Aloud here at Pop Princesses HQ. We love her sassy attitude and her sense of style and amazing hair!

Star!

1. Jessie J

What a rise to the top! Jessie J is our Ultimate Pop Princess. After working hard as a writer and overcoming some major obstacles Jessie J has become a worldwide success almost overnight. With her role as a coach on The Voice UK it seems she is here to stay and we can't wait for the next chapter in her story.

So cool!